MAD LIBS®
THE BIG BANG THEORY MAD LIBS

by Laura Marchesani

PRICE STERN SLOAN
An Imprint of Penguin Random House

PRICE STERN SLOAN
An Imprint of Penguin Random House LLC

Mad Libs format copyright © 2015 by Price Stern Sloan,
an imprint of Penguin Random House LLC. All rights reserved.

Concept created by Roger Price & Leonard Stern

Published by Price Stern Sloan, an imprint of Penguin Random House LLC,
345 Hudson Street, New York, New York 10014.
Printed in the USA.

ISBN 978-0-399-54217-6
1 3 5 7 9 10 8 6 4 2

MAD LIBS® is a game for people who don't like games! It can be played by one, two, three, four, or forty.

• RIDICULOUSLY SIMPLE DIRECTIONS

In this tablet you will find stories containing blank spaces where words are left out. One player, the READER, selects one of these stories. The READER does not tell anyone what the story is about. Instead, he/she asks the other players, the WRITERS, to give him/her words. These words are used to fill in the blank spaces in the story.

• TO PLAY

The READER asks each WRITER in turn to call out a word—an adjective or a noun or whatever the space calls for—and uses them to fill in the blank spaces in the story. The result is a MAD LIBS® game.

When the READER then reads the completed MAD LIBS® game to the other players, they will discover that they have written a story that is fantastic, screamingly funny, shocking, silly, crazy, or just plain dumb—depending upon which words each WRITER called out.

• EXAMPLE (*Before* and *After*)

" _____ !" he said _____
        EXCLAMATION   ADVERB

as he jumped into his convertible _____ and
                                                NOUN

drove off with his _____ wife.
                            ADJECTIVE

" _____*Ouch*_____ !" he said _____*stupidly*_____
        EXCLAMATION   ADVERB

as he jumped into his convertible _____*cat*_____ and
                                                NOUN

drove off with his _____*brave*_____ wife.
                            ADJECTIVE

In case you have forgotten what adjectives, adverbs, nouns, and verbs are, here is a quick review:

An **ADJECTIVE** describes something or somebody. *Lumpy, soft, ugly, messy,* and *short* are adjectives.

An **ADVERB** tells how something is done. It modifies a verb and usually ends in "ly." *Modestly, stupidly, greedily,* and *carefully* are adverbs.

A **NOUN** is the name of a person, place, or thing. *Sidewalk, umbrella, bridle, bathtub,* and *nose* are nouns.

A **VERB** is an action word. *Run, pitch, jump,* and *swim* are verbs. Put the verbs in past tense if the directions say PAST TENSE. *Ran, pitched, jumped,* and *swam* are verbs in the past tense.

When we ask for **A PLACE**, we mean any sort of place: a country or city (*Spain, Cleveland*) or a room (*bathroom, kitchen*).

An **EXCLAMATION** or **SILLY WORD** is any sort of funny sound, gasp, grunt, or outcry, like *Wow!, Ouch!, Whomp!, Ick!,* and *Gadzooks!*

When we ask for specific words, like a **NUMBER**, a **COLOR**, an **ANIMAL**, or a **PART OF THE BODY**, we mean a word that is one of those things, like *seven, blue, horse,* or *head.*

When we ask for a **PLURAL**, it means more than one. For example, *cat* pluralized is *cats.*

MAD LIBS® is fun to play with friends, but you can also play it by yourself! To begin with, DO NOT look at the story on the page below. Fill in the blanks on this page with the words called for. Then, using the words you have selected, fill in the blank spaces in the story.

Now you've created your own hilarious MAD LIBS® game!

PENNY AND LEONARD: A LOVE STORY

ADJECTIVE _____

A PLACE _____

PART OF THE BODY _____

ADJECTIVE _____

ADJECTIVE _____

A PLACE _____

VERB (PAST TENSE) _____

VERB _____

NOUN _____

VERB ENDING IN "ING" _____

ADJECTIVE _____

ADJECTIVE _____

VERB _____

NOUN _____

NUMBER _____

ADJECTIVE _____

ADVERB _____

ANIMAL (PLURAL) _____

MAD LIBS
PENNY AND LEONARD: A LOVE STORY

When Leonard met Penny, she was just another _____ girl
ADJECTIVE

who lived across (the) _____ from him. At first he tried to
A PLACE

catch Penny's _____ by doing lots of _____ favors
PART OF THE BODY   ADJECTIVE

for her. Eventually, all that _____ work paid off when he
ADJECTIVE

returned from an expedition to (the) _____ and the two of
A PLACE

them finally _____. Their relationship ended when Penny
VERB (PAST TENSE)

couldn't say "I _____ you," so Leonard went on to date
VERB

Raj's _____, Priya. Eventually, Leonard and Penny got back
NOUN

together, but Leonard blew it by proposing to Penny in bed after they

just finished _____! Talk about a/an _____
VERB ENDING IN "ING"   ADJECTIVE

idea. But in the end, their _____ relationship blossomed,
ADJECTIVE

and Penny asked Leonard to _____ her. Luckily, Leonard had
VERB

been carrying a/an _____ in his wallet for _____
NOUN   NUMBER

years—he was just waiting for the _____ moment! It's
ADJECTIVE

_____ ever after for these two love-_____.
ADVERB   ANIMAL (PLURAL)

MAD LIBS® is fun to play with friends, but you can also play it by yourself! To begin with, DO NOT look at the story on the page below. Fill in the blanks on this page with the words called for. Then, using the words you have selected, fill in the blank spaces in the story.

Now you've created your own hilarious MAD LIBS® game!

THE ROOMMATE AGREEMENT

PLURAL NOUN _____

ADJECTIVE _____

VERB _____

NOUN _____

A PLACE _____

ADJECTIVE _____

PLURAL NOUN _____

OCCUPATION _____

VERB _____

TYPE OF FOOD (PLURAL) _____

NOUN _____

NOUN _____

ADJECTIVE _____

TYPE OF LIQUID _____

NUMBER _____

SILLY WORD _____

MAD LIBS
THE ROOMMATE AGREEMENT

Here are some notable _____ from Sheldon and Leonard's
                          PLURAL NOUN

_____ Roommate Agreement:
ADJECTIVE

The Skynet Clause: Leonard will help Sheldon _____ an
                                                   VERB

Artificial _____ that Sheldon created and is now taking over
            NOUN

(the) _____.
       A PLACE

Section 37B, _____ Duties: Leonard will assist Sheldon in his
                ADJECTIVE

various _____, including driving Sheldon to the _____.
         PLURAL NOUN   OCCUPATION

Leonard must also provide a "confirmation _____" to discern
                                            VERB

whether various _____ are still edible.
                 TYPE OF FOOD (PLURAL)

Section 74C: Leonard must assist Sheldon if he ever becomes a/an

_____.
  NOUN

Addendum J: When Sheldon uses the _____ second, any
                                        NOUN

and all measures will be taken to ensure a/an _____ supply
                                                ADJECTIVE

of hot _____.
        TYPE OF LIQUID

Section 8, Subsection C, Paragraph 4: Roommates shall give

_____-hour notice of impending _____.
  NUMBER   SILLY WORD

From THE BIG BANG THEORY MAD LIBS® • Copyright © 2015 Warner Bros. Entertainment Inc. THE BIG
BANG THEORY and all related characters and elements are trademarks of and © Warner Bros. Entertainment Inc. (s15)
Published by Price Stern Sloan, an imprint of Penguin Random House LLC, 345 Hudson Street, New York, NY 10014.

MAD LIBS® is fun to play with friends, but you can also play it by yourself! To begin with, DO NOT look at the story on the page below. Fill in the blanks on this page with the words called for. Then, using the words you have selected, fill in the blank spaces in the story.

Now you've created your own hilarious MAD LIBS® game!

HOW TO BE A GOOD SON, BY HOWARD

ADJECTIVE _____

NUMBER _____

A PLACE _____

PART OF THE BODY _____

ADVERB _____

TYPE OF FOOD _____

SAME TYPE OF FOOD _____

ADJECTIVE _____

PART OF THE BODY _____

ARTICLE OF CLOTHING _____

PERSON IN ROOM _____

TYPE OF LIQUID _____

NUMBER _____

ADJECTIVE _____

VERB _____

PLURAL NOUN _____

MAD LIBS®
HOW TO BE A GOOD SON,
BY HOWARD

It's not always _____ to be the #_____ son in the
⎯⎯⎯⎯ ADJECTIVE ⎯⎯⎯⎯⎯⎯ NUMBER

entire _____. If you want to earn a place in your mother's
⎯⎯⎯ A PLACE

_____ for all of eternity, here are a few things you should
PART OF THE BODY

_____ do:
ADVERB

- Always eat her _____ and ask for seconds, even if the
⎯⎯⎯⎯ TYPE OF FOOD

  _____ is more _____ than your great-aunt's
  SAME TYPE OF FOOD ⎯⎯⎯⎯ ADJECTIVE

  _____.
  PART OF THE BODY

- Never complain when you're asked to take her _____
  ⎯⎯⎯⎯ ARTICLE OF CLOTHING

  shopping—or pawn the responsibility off on some other sucker, like

  _____.
  PERSON IN ROOM

- Bathe her with warm _____ at least _____
  ⎯⎯⎯ TYPE OF LIQUID ⎯⎯⎯ NUMBER

  times a week.

- She likes doing _____ things for you and your friends, so
  ⎯⎯⎯ ADJECTIVE

  make sure to _____ at her really loudly every time a guest
  VERB

  comes over to bring up a plate of _____ to snack on.
  ⎯⎯⎯ PLURAL NOUN

From THE BIG BANG THEORY MAD LIBS® • Copyright © 2015 Warner Bros. Entertainment Inc. THE BIG
BANG THEORY and all related characters and elements are trademarks of and © Warner Bros. Entertainment Inc. (s15)
Published by Price Stern Sloan, an imprint of Penguin Random House LLC, 345 Hudson Street, New York, NY 10014.

MAD LIBS® is fun to play with friends, but you can also play it by yourself! To begin with, DO NOT look at the story on the page below. Fill in the blanks on this page with the words called for. Then, using the words you have selected, fill in the blank spaces in the story.

Now you've created your own hilarious MAD LIBS® game!

HOW TO GET THE GIRL: A GUIDE, BY LEONARD

NUMBER _____

NOUN _____

SAME NOUN _____

ADJECTIVE _____

PART OF THE BODY _____

VERB _____

ADJECTIVE _____

ADJECTIVE _____

ADJECTIVE _____

NOUN _____

ADJECTIVE _____

NUMBER _____

ADJECTIVE _____

A PLACE _____

ADJECTIVE _____

ADJECTIVE _____

NOUN _____

NUMBER _____

MAD LIBS®
HOW TO GET THE GIRL: A GUIDE, BY LEONARD

It only took _____ years, but Leonard finally landed the
        NUMBER

_____ of his dreams: Penny. If you want to lock down your
NOUN

own dream-_____, follow Leonard's _____ advice:
      SAME NOUN   ADJECTIVE

• Be a/an _____ to _____ on. Comforting her
       PART OF THE BODY   VERB

in her _____ time of need will make you look like a/an
      ADJECTIVE

_____ guy!
ADJECTIVE

• Support her dreams, no matter how _____ they might
                       ADJECTIVE

be. Never insult her for not having a/an _____ degree and
                         NOUN

a/an _____ job, or only reading books like _____
    ADJECTIVE   NUMBER

Days to _____ *Abs*!
      ADJECTIVE

• Be as romantic as possible. When you go on an expedition

to (the) _____, bring back a/an _____
      A PLACE   ADJECTIVE

snowflake encased in glass, because what could possibly be more

_____ than that?!
ADJECTIVE

• Buy an engagement _____, just in case, and then be patient
                 NOUN

when you have to wait _____ years to give it to her!
                  NUMBER

MAD LIBS® is fun to play with friends, but you can also play it by yourself! To begin with, DO NOT look at the story on the page below. Fill in the blanks on this page with the words called for. Then, using the words you have selected, fill in the blank spaces in the story.

Now you've created your own hilarious MAD LIBS® game!

TAKEOUT-NIGHT ETIQUETTE

FIRST NAME (MALE) _____

ADJECTIVE _____

NOUN _____

TYPE OF FOOD _____

VERB _____

ANIMAL _____

NUMBER _____

COLOR _____

ADJECTIVE _____

NOUN _____

PERSON IN ROOM (MALE) _____

VERB ENDING IN "ING" _____

VERB _____

NOUN _____

ADJECTIVE _____

MAD LIBS®

TAKEOUT-NIGHT ETIQUETTE

Takeout night at Sheldon and _____'s apartment can be a
                              FIRST NAME (MALE)

very _____ dining experience, if you follow all the rules.
       ADJECTIVE

Each type of _____ has its own designated day. Don't
              NOUN

come over expecting to eat _____ on a Tuesday, because
                           TYPE OF FOOD

it's just not happening. Also, only certain restaurants are acceptable

to _____ from. Szechuan Palace is the only place Sheldon
   VERB

will order cashew _____ from—even though it closed down
                  ANIMAL

_____ years ago, so they have been ordering from _____
NUMBER   COLOR

Dragon instead. Each guest has his or her own designated seat.

Attempt to steal Sheldon's _____ spot at your own risk!
                           ADJECTIVE

And finally, always make sure to pay your _____—that is,
                                          NOUN

unless you're Penny, and _____ always offers! If you
                         PERSON IN ROOM (MALE)

feel like _____ out, make sure it's on the third Thursday
          VERB ENDING IN "ING"

of every month, which is known as "Anything Can _____
                                                VERB

Thursday." Otherwise you might wind up eating spaghetti with cut-

up _____ pieces for dinner. A/An _____ meal—
   NOUN   ADJECTIVE

unless you're Sheldon!

MAD LIBS® is fun to play with friends, but you can also play it by yourself! To begin with, DO NOT look at the story on the page below. Fill in the blanks on this page with the words called for. Then, using the words you have selected, fill in the blank spaces in the story.

Now you've created your own hilarious MAD LIBS® game!

AN IDIOT'S GUIDE TO STRING THEORY

NOUN _____

OCCUPATION _____

VERB ENDING IN "ING" _____

ADJECTIVE _____

PLURAL NOUN _____

NUMBER _____

PLURAL NOUN _____

VERB _____

ADJECTIVE _____

ADJECTIVE _____

COLOR _____

NOUN _____

ADJECTIVE _____

EXCLAMATION _____

ADJECTIVE _____

PART OF THE BODY _____

MAD LIBS®
AN IDIOT'S GUIDE TO
STRING THEORY

Have you ever wondered what _____ theory actually is?
                                    NOUN

It doesn't take a rocket _____ to figure it out—after all,
                              OCCUPATION

Howard has a/an _____ understanding of it, and he's only
                   VERB ENDING IN "ING"

a/an _____ engineer! In string theory, the _____ of
        ADJECTIVE   PLURAL NOUN

particle physics are replaced by _____-dimensional objects
                                        NUMBER

called strings. String theory explains how these _____
                                                      PLURAL NOUN

_____ through space and interact with one another. It's
      VERB

a/an _____ way to address the deep and _____
        ADJECTIVE   ADJECTIVE

questions of fundamental physics. It can be used to solve problems

in subjects like _____-hole physics, condensed _____
                      COLOR   NOUN

physics, and _____ universe cosmology. _____!
                  ADJECTIVE   EXCLAMATION

String theory seems more _____ than we thought. Maybe
                              ADJECTIVE

Howard has an intelligent _____, after all!
                            PART OF THE BODY

MAD LIBS® is fun to play with friends, but you can also play it by yourself! To begin with, DO NOT look at the story on the page below. Fill in the blanks on this page with the words called for. Then, using the words you have selected, fill in the blank spaces in the story.

Now you've created your own hilarious MAD LIBS® game!

HOWARD IN SPACE

ADJECTIVE _____

NOUN _____

ADJECTIVE _____

NUMBER _____

A PLACE _____

VERB _____

ADJECTIVE _____

ADJECTIVE _____

ADJECTIVE _____

NOUN _____

ADJECTIVE _____

SAME ADJECTIVE _____

VERB ENDING IN "ING" _____

OCCUPATION _____

ADJECTIVE _____

A PLACE _____

MAD LIBS®

HOWARD IN SPACE

Did I ever tell you about that one _____ time I went to
                                    ADJECTIVE

outer _____? It was totally _____, but I'm sure
        NOUN   ADJECTIVE

that doesn't surprise you—it is space, after all. First we trained for

_____ days in (the) _____ to _____
    NUMBER   A PLACE   VERB

for our trip. But no _____ training can ever really prepare
                        ADJECTIVE

you for what lies in the _____ beyond. The other astronauts
                            ADJECTIVE

and I really bonded—I even earned a/an _____ nickname:
                                            ADJECTIVE

_____ Loops. Funny, right? When we took off, I was a
    NOUN

little _____—not going to lie about that. Who wouldn't be
        ADJECTIVE

_____?! But by the time we reached _____
SAME ADJECTIVE   VERB ENDING IN "ING"

altitude, I felt like a total _____. I couldn't wait to call
                                OCCUPATION

Bernie and my mother and tell them what a/an _____ time
                                                ADJECTIVE

I was having in (the) _____!
                        A PLACE

From THE BIG BANG THEORY MAD LIBS® • Copyright © 2015 Warner Bros. Entertainment Inc. THE BIG
BANG THEORY and all related characters and elements are trademarks of and © Warner Bros. Entertainment Inc. (s15)
Published by Price Stern Sloan, an imprint of Penguin Random House LLC, 345 Hudson Street, New York, NY 10014.

MAD LIBS® is fun to play with friends, but you can also play it by yourself! To begin with, DO NOT look at the story on the page below. Fill in the blanks on this page with the words called for. Then, using the words you have selected, fill in the blank spaces in the story.

Now you've created your own hilarious MAD LIBS® game!

FUN WITH FLAGS

ADJECTIVE _____

OCCUPATION _____

PLURAL NOUN _____

NUMBER _____

ADJECTIVE _____

SILLY WORD _____

SAME SILLY WORD _____

PLURAL NOUN _____

EXCLAMATION _____

VERB ENDING IN "ING" _____

PLURAL NOUN _____

NUMBER _____

ANIMAL _____

ADJECTIVE _____

NOUN _____

NOUN _____

NOUN _____

ADJECTIVE _____

MAD LIBS®

FUN WITH FLAGS

Here's an excerpt from the premiere episode of Sheldon's
_____ podcast, *Fun with Flags*!
<small>ADJECTIVE</small>

Sheldon: Hi, I'm _____ Sheldon Cooper, and welcome
<small>OCCUPATION</small>

to the premiere episode of *Fun with* _____. Over the next
<small>PLURAL NOUN</small>

_____ weeks, we are going to explore the _____
<small>NUMBER</small> <small>ADJECTIVE</small>

world of _____.
<small>SILLY WORD</small>

Amy: Hang on, Dr. C. What's _____?
<small>SAME SILLY WORD</small>

Sheldon: It's the study of _____.
<small>PLURAL NOUN</small>

Amy: _____! I think I just learned something. And I had
<small>EXCLAMATION</small>

fun while _____ it.
<small>VERB ENDING IN "ING"</small>

Sheldon: Fun and _____ are two sides to this video podcast,
<small>PLURAL NOUN</small>

not unlike the only _____-sided state flag, Oregon. Oh,
<small>NUMBER</small>

look. Hello, Mr. _____! In future episodes, we'll answer
<small>ANIMAL</small>

some _____ questions. What's the only non-rectangular
<small>ADJECTIVE</small>

_____? What _____ appears second most often
<small>NOUN</small> <small>NOUN</small>

on flags? And so on. Amy, why are you waving a white _____?
<small>NOUN</small>

Amy: I'm surrendering to _____ fun!
<small>ADJECTIVE</small>

MAD LIBS® is fun to play with friends, but you can also play it by yourself! To begin with, DO NOT look at the story on the page below. Fill in the blanks on this page with the words called for. Then, using the words you have selected, fill in the blank spaces in the story.

Now you've created your own hilarious MAD LIBS® game!

EMILY OR CINNAMON?

ADJECTIVE _____

ANIMAL _____

PLURAL NOUN _____

PART OF THE BODY _____

VERB ENDING IN "ING" _____

NOUN _____

SILLY WORD _____

ADJECTIVE _____

ADJECTIVE _____

TYPE OF FOOD _____

PART OF THE BODY _____

MAD LIBS®

EMILY OR CINNAMON?

It's no secret that there are two _____ women in Raj's life—
                                    ADJECTIVE

his girlfriend, Emily, and his pet _____, Cinnamon. Both
                                    ANIMAL

of these _____ have stolen Raj's _____, but it can
          PLURAL NOUN   PART OF THE BODY

sometimes get a little confusing when he's _____ on and
                                            VERB ENDING IN "ING"

on about the _____ of his life. So which one is he talking
                NOUN

about here—Emily or Cinnamon?

- "Don't be scared, _____; it's only thunder." (Answer:
                       SILLY WORD

  Cinnamon)

- "Looks like I found your _____ spot!" (Answer: Emily)
                            ADJECTIVE

- "I had the most _____ dream about you last night."
                    ADJECTIVE

  (Answer: Cinnamon)

- "I'd give you a bite, but you know you're not supposed to have

  _____." (Answer: Cinnamon)
   TYPE OF FOOD

- "Of course I want your kisses. Let me brush my _____
                                                  PART OF THE BODY

  first." (Answer: Emily)

MAD LIBS® is fun to play with friends, but you can also play it by yourself! To begin with, DO NOT look at the story on the page below. Fill in the blanks on this page with the words called for. Then, using the words you have selected, fill in the blank spaces in the story.

Now you've created your own hilarious MAD LIBS® game!

PENNY'S RÉSUMÉ

VERB ENDING IN "ING" _____

TYPE OF FOOD _____

ADJECTIVE _____

CELEBRITY (FEMALE) _____

VERB ENDING IN "ING" _____

FIRST NAME (FEMALE) _____

ADJECTIVE _____

ADJECTIVE _____

NOUN _____

VERB ENDING IN "ING" _____

ADJECTIVE _____

ANIMAL _____

VERB ENDING IN "ING" _____

NOUN _____

ARTICLE OF CLOTHING _____

MAD LIBS®

PENNY'S RÉSUMÉ

When Penny's not busy _____ at the _____
VERB ENDING IN "ING"   TYPE OF FOOD

Factory, she's trying to become a/an _____ actress
ADJECTIVE

just like _____. Here are some of her impressive
CELEBRITY (FEMALE)

_____ credits:
VERB ENDING IN "ING"

- The role of _____ in the musical *Rent*: Even though
FIRST NAME (FEMALE)

  she's a/an _____ singer, Penny still landed the gig for this
ADJECTIVE

  _____ musical.
ADJECTIVE

- Anne Frank: Penny plays the _____ Anne Frank in a
NOUN

  theater located above a/an _____ alley.
VERB ENDING IN "ING"

- Hemorrhoid girl: Penny lands a/an _____ role as a girl
ADJECTIVE

  riding a/an _____ in a hemorrhoid commercial.
ANIMAL

- *Serial Ape-ist*: Penny lands the _____ role in
VERB ENDING IN "ING"

  this low-budget _____ film—and even takes her
NOUN

  _____ off for a shower scene!
ARTICLE OF CLOTHING

MAD LIBS® is fun to play with friends, but you can also play it by yourself! To begin with, DO NOT look at the story on the page below. Fill in the blanks on this page with the words called for. Then, using the words you have selected, fill in the blank spaces in the story.

Now you've created your own hilarious MAD LIBS® game!

GIRLS' NIGHT WITH PENNY, AMY, AND BERNADETTE

ADJECTIVE _____

ADJECTIVE _____

ADVERB _____

PART OF THE BODY _____

PLURAL NOUN _____

ADJECTIVE _____

PART OF THE BODY _____

NOUN _____

A PLACE _____

VERB _____

NOUN _____

VERB _____

ADJECTIVE _____

MAD LIBS®
GIRLS' NIGHT WITH PENNY, AMY, AND BERNADETTE

Girls' night at Penny's apartment is always a/an _____ time.

ADJECTIVE

Here's a sample of one of their _____ conversations:

ADJECTIVE

Amy: So, long story short, turns out I have a/an _____ firm

ADVERB

_____.

PART OF THE BODY

Penny: You know, Amy, when we say girl talk, it doesn't always have to

be about our lady _____.

PLURAL NOUN

Amy: Shame. I have a/an _____ zinger about my tilted

ADJECTIVE

_____.

PART OF THE BODY

Penny: So where should we go tonight? A bar? A/An _____?

NOUN

(The) _____?

A PLACE

Amy: We could just stay here and continue to _____.

VERB

I have a feeling that after tonight, one of you will become my best

_____ forever. Or BFF, if you _____. Which I

NOUN   VERB

don't.

. . . And the rest is _____ history!

ADJECTIVE

From THE BIG BANG THEORY MAD LIBS® • Copyright © 2015 Warner Bros. Entertainment Inc. THE BIG
BANG THEORY and all related characters and elements are trademarks of and © Warner Bros. Entertainment Inc. (s15)
Published by Price Stern Sloan, an imprint of Penguin Random House LLC, 345 Hudson Street, New York, NY 10014.

MAD LIBS® is fun to play with friends, but you can also play it by yourself! To begin with, DO NOT look at the story on the page below. Fill in the blanks on this page with the words called for. Then, using the words you have selected, fill in the blank spaces in the story.

Now you've created your own hilarious MAD LIBS® game!

UNLUCKY IN LOVE

PLURAL NOUN _____

ADJECTIVE _____

COLOR _____

ADJECTIVE _____

FIRST NAME (FEMALE) _____

ARTICLE OF CLOTHING (PLURAL) _____

NUMBER _____

OCCUPATION _____

PART OF THE BODY _____

NOUN _____

NOUN _____

ADJECTIVE _____

A PLACE _____

PLURAL NOUN _____

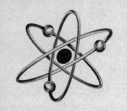

MAD LIBS®

UNLUCKY IN LOVE

Raj, Howard, and Leonard are lucky enough to have found the

_____ of their dreams, but it wasn't always like that. In fact,
PLURAL NOUN

the guys had a lot of _____ luck with the ladies and struck
ADJECTIVE

out more often than not. Who could forget . . . ?

- When Raj and Howard dressed in all _____ and
COLOR

  pretended to be _____ goths just to pick up girls?
  ADJECTIVE

- When Leonard dated Raj's sister, _____, and she
FIRST NAME (FEMALE)

  dressed him in fancy _____?
  ARTICLE OF CLOTHING (PLURAL)

- When Leonard, Raj, and Howard were almost tricked into having

  a/an _____-way with a visiting _____?
  NUMBER   OCCUPATION

- When Howard got his _____ stuck in a mechanical
PART OF THE BODY

  _____?
  NOUN

- When Raj dated a/an _____ who couldn't speak and
NOUN

  was even more _____ than him, so he took her to (the)
  ADJECTIVE

  _____ for their first date?
  A PLACE

- When Howard and Leslie became _____ with benefits?
PLURAL NOUN

MAD LIBS® is fun to play with friends, but you can also play it by yourself! To begin with, DO NOT look at the story on the page below. Fill in the blanks on this page with the words called for. Then, using the words you have selected, fill in the blank spaces in the story.

Now you've created your own hilarious MAD LIBS® game!

A NIGHT AT THE CHEESECAKE FACTORY

OCCUPATION _____

ARTICLE OF CLOTHING _____

NOUN _____

ADJECTIVE _____

NOUN _____

SAME NOUN _____

TYPE OF LIQUID _____

PLURAL NOUN _____

ADJECTIVE _____

NOUN _____

TYPE OF FOOD _____

A PLACE _____

VERB ENDING IN "ING" _____

ADJECTIVE _____

PLURAL NOUN _____

NOUN _____

MAD LIBS
A NIGHT AT THE
CHEESECAKE FACTORY

What is a typical night at the Cheesecake Factory like for

_____ Penny? First, she has to put on her best green and
<u>OCCUPATION</u>

yellow _____ with suspenders and a matching frilly
<u>ARTICLE OF CLOTHING</u>

_____. On Tuesday nights, Leonard, Raj, and Howard come
<u>NOUN</u>

to eat, and taking their orders is _____ business. Sheldon
<u>ADJECTIVE</u>

always orders the same meal: a barbeque _____ cheeseburger
<u>NOUN</u>

(barbeque, _____, and cheese on the side). Raj prefers the
<u>SAME NOUN</u>

_____-battered fish and _____, while Leonard
<u>TYPE OF LIQUID</u>   <u>PLURAL NOUN</u>

sometimes orders the Factory Burrito _____ (without cheese
<u>ADJECTIVE</u>

and sour cream, of course, thanks to his _____ intolerance).
<u>NOUN</u>

Penny enjoys eavesdropping on other people's conversations by

bringing _____ to their tables. Or, if she's working at the
<u>TYPE OF FOOD</u>

bar, it's even easier—she just makes a/an _____ iced tea, and
<u>A PLACE</u>

the secrets usually come _____ out! Working at the
<u>VERB ENDING IN "ING"</u>

Cheesecake Factory is a/an _____ job, but it's clear that Penny
<u>ADJECTIVE</u>

is better suited for other _____—like acting or _____
<u>PLURAL NOUN</u>   <u>NOUN</u>

sales!

From THE BIG BANG THEORY MAD LIBS® • Copyright © 2015 Warner Bros. Entertainment Inc. THE BIG
BANG THEORY and all related characters and elements are trademarks of and © Warner Bros. Entertainment Inc. (s15)
Published by Price Stern Sloan, an imprint of Penguin Random House LLC, 345 Hudson Street, New York, NY 10014.

MAD LIBS® is fun to play with friends, but you can also play it by yourself! To begin with, DO NOT look at the story on the page below. Fill in the blanks on this page with the words called for. Then, using the words you have selected, fill in the blank spaces in the story.

Now you've created your own hilarious MAD LIBS® game!

BESTIES

PLURAL NOUN _____

NOUN _____

ADJECTIVE _____

ADVERB _____

ADJECTIVE _____

VERB _____

ADJECTIVE _____

ADVERB _____

ADJECTIVE _____

ADJECTIVE _____

PLURAL NOUN _____

NUMBER _____

ADJECTIVE _____

PART OF THE BODY _____

VERB _____

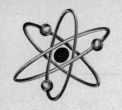

MAD LIBS

BESTIES

Everyone knows that Amy, Penny, and Bernadette are besties—

best _____ forever. At least, according to Amy, that is.
　　　　　PLURAL NOUN

After having a sleepover at Penny's _____, Amy officially
　　　　　　　　　　　　　　　　　　NOUN

declared the three of them to be _____ friends for life. Amy
　　　　　　　　　　　　　　　ADJECTIVE

_____ worships the ground Penny walks on, and tries to fit in
ADVERB

with her in any way possible. She even tried wearing _____
　　　　　　　　　　　　　　　　　　　　　　　ADJECTIVE

heels to be more like Penny, despite the fact that Amy couldn't even

_____ in them! Amy's feelings toward Bernadette are a little
VERB

less _____. She _____ considers Bernadette to
　　ADJECTIVE　　　　　ADVERB

be the least cool and the least _____ of their group. Amy
　　　　　　　　　　　　　　ADJECTIVE

shows her love for her friends in _____ ways, like giving
　　　　　　　　　　　　　　ADJECTIVE

the girls friendship _____ to wear and buying Penny a/an
　　　　　　　PLURAL NOUN

$_____ oil painting for her birthday. Even though she might
　NUMBER

come across a little _____, Amy has a/an _____
　　　　　　　ADJECTIVE　　　　　　　　PART OF THE BODY

of gold. Just don't mess with her friends—then she'll have to

_____ you!
VERB

MAD LIBS® is fun to play with friends, but you can also play it by yourself! To begin with, DO NOT look at the story on the page below. Fill in the blanks on this page with the words called for. Then, using the words you have selected, fill in the blank spaces in the story.

Now you've created your own hilarious MAD LIBS® game!

GEEKING OUT

ADJECTIVE _____

ADJECTIVE _____

ADJECTIVE _____

COLOR _____

ADJECTIVE _____

PERSON IN ROOM _____

PLURAL NOUN _____

ANIMAL _____

A PLACE _____

NOUN _____

NOUN _____

PLURAL NOUN _____

NOUN _____

SAME NOUN _____

SAME NOUN _____

ADJECTIVE _____

FIRST NAME (MALE) _____

SILLY WORD _____

MAD LIBS®

GEEKING OUT

Sheldon, Leonard, Raj, and Howard have lots of _____
                                                    ADJECTIVE

interests, that's for sure. On any given night of the week, chances are

_____ that you could catch them doing one of the following:
  ADJECTIVE

• Solving complex, _____ equations with the help of their
                        ADJECTIVE

  trusty _____-board. Bonus points if it leads to a/an
              COLOR

  _____ argument about who is right: _____ or
      ADJECTIVE   PERSON IN ROOM

  everyone else.

• Playing games. Favorites include Dungeons and _____;
                                                      PLURAL NOUN

  Rock, Paper, Scissors, _____, Spock; The Settlers of (the)
                              ANIMAL

  _____; 3-D chess; and video games like _____.
      A PLACE   NOUN

• Obsessing over their favorite _____ franchises, like
                                      NOUN

  The Lord of the _____, _____ Wars, and
                      PLURAL NOUN   NOUN

  _____ Trek. As Penny would say, "One of those
      SAME NOUN

  _____ things!"
      SAME NOUN

• Worshipping some of their _____ icons and heroes, like
                                  ADJECTIVE

  _____ Lucas, Stan Lee, and Sheldon's favorite, Leonard
  FIRST NAME (MALE)

  _____.
      SILLY WORD

MAD LIBS® is fun to play with friends, but you can also play it by yourself! To begin with, DO NOT look at the story on the page below. Fill in the blanks on this page with the words called for. Then, using the words you have selected, fill in the blank spaces in the story.

Now you've created your own hilarious MAD LIBS® game!

BARRY IS THE BEST

ADVERB _____

OCCUPATION _____

A PLACE _____

NOUN _____

ADJECTIVE _____

PERSON IN ROOM (MALE) _____

ADJECTIVE _____

ADJECTIVE _____

VERB _____

PLURAL NOUN _____

NOUN _____

CELEBRITY (FEMALE) _____

NOUN _____

ADJECTIVE _____

NOUN _____

VERB ENDING IN "ING" _____

NOUN _____

ADJECTIVE _____

MAD LIBS®

BARRY IS THE BEST

Barry Kripke is _____ convinced that he is the best
                         ADVERB

_____ at (the) _____. He even decided to
  OCCUPATION   A PLACE

quit working as a/an _____ scientist and become a
                            NOUN

string theorist just to prove how much more _____
                                                    ADJECTIVE

he is than _____. Barry has had his fair share of
            PERSON IN ROOM (MALE)

_____ arguments with Sheldon, Raj, Howard, and Leonard.
  ADJECTIVE

He built a/an _____ robot, the Kripke Krippler, just to
                   ADJECTIVE

_____ against the guys' robot, MONTE. He's also pulled
  VERB

some epic _____ over the years, like the time he pumped
             PLURAL NOUN

_____ gas into Sheldon's office so his voice sounded like
  NOUN

_____ during a/an _____ interview. Barry
  CELEBRITY (FEMALE)   NOUN

thinks he's better than the guys in every _____ way, which
                                                 ADJECTIVE

includes his taste in women—in fact, he still can't understand what

Leonard sees in his _____, Roxanne. So what if Siri can't
                          NOUN

understand his _____? When you're a world-famous
                  VERB ENDING IN "ING"

_____, those are just _____ details!
  NOUN   ADJECTIVE

MAD LIBS® is fun to play with friends, but you can also play it by yourself! To begin with, DO NOT look at the story on the page below. Fill in the blanks on this page with the words called for. Then, using the words you have selected, fill in the blank spaces in the story.

Now you've created your own hilarious MAD LIBS® game!

AMY'S FANFICTION

ADJECTIVE _____

ADJECTIVE _____

NOUN _____

OCCUPATION _____

NOUN _____

ADJECTIVE _____

ADJECTIVE _____

VERB _____

NOUN _____

ADJECTIVE _____

PART OF THE BODY (PLURAL) _____

ADJECTIVE _____

VERB ENDING IN "ING" _____

NOUN _____

PART OF THE BODY _____

PLURAL NOUN _____

MAD LIBS®

AMY'S FANFICTION

Here is a/an _____ excerpt from Amy's _____ *House*

ADJECTIVE ADJECTIVE

on the Prairie fanfiction, titled *Amelia and the* _____ *-Traveling*

NOUN

_____.

OCCUPATION

It was just past dawn on the _____, and like every morning,

NOUN

Amelia prepared to do her _____ chores. Except

ADJECTIVE

something about this morning felt _____. Maybe it

ADJECTIVE

was the first _____ of winter in the _____, or

VERB NOUN

maybe it was the unconscious _____ man with porcelain

ADJECTIVE

_____ and _____ clothing that

PART OF THE BODY (PLURAL) ADJECTIVE

she was about to discover _____ in the field—

VERB ENDING IN "ING"

a/an _____ who would open her _____ to new

NOUN PART OF THE BODY

possibilities and her body to new _____.

PLURAL NOUN

MAD LIBS® is fun to play with friends, but you can also play it by yourself! To begin with, DO NOT look at the story on the page below. Fill in the blanks on this page with the words called for. Then, using the words you have selected, fill in the blank spaces in the story.

Now you've created your own hilarious MAD LIBS® game!

BAZINGA!

ADJECTIVE _____

NOUN _____

NOUN _____

ADJECTIVE _____

ADJECTIVE _____

VERB ENDING IN "ING" _____

ADJECTIVE _____

ADJECTIVE _____

NOUN _____

ADVERB _____

ADJECTIVE _____

NOUN _____

ADJECTIVE _____

MAD LIBS®

BAZINGA!

When something _____ happens, Sheldon's go-to word is
              ADJECTIVE

BAZINGA! It's the perfect _____ for any situation, whether
                   NOUN

you're pranking a/an _____ or making a/an _____
              NOUN   ADJECTIVE

joke at someone's expense. Here's a list of some of Sheldon's most

_____ BAZINGA! moments.
 ADJECTIVE

- After Sheldon suggests that maybe he and Amy try

  _____ at least once just to see what it's like, he gives
  VERB ENDING IN "ING"

  her a/an _____ BAZINGA!
         ADJECTIVE

- In an attempt to solve a/an _____ physics problem,
                 ADJECTIVE

  Sheldon sneaks out to a/an _____ pit in the middle of
              NOUN

  the night and jumps around shouting BAZINGA! as Leonard

  _____ tries to catch him.
   ADVERB

- When Sheldon gets totally _____ in order to get onstage
                ADJECTIVE

  and accept a/an _____, he gives a/an _____
           NOUN   ADJECTIVE

  and offensive speech filled with BAZINGAS!

From THE BIG BANG THEORY MAD LIBS® • Copyright © 2015 Warner Bros. Entertainment Inc. THE BIG
BANG THEORY and all related characters and elements are trademarks of and © Warner Bros. Entertainment Inc. (s15)
Published by Price Stern Sloan, an imprint of Penguin Random House LLC, 345 Hudson Street, New York, NY 10014.

MAD LIBS® is fun to play with friends, but you can also play it by yourself! To begin with, DO NOT look at the story on the page below. Fill in the blanks on this page with the words called for. Then, using the words you have selected, fill in the blank spaces in the story.

Now you've created your own hilarious MAD LIBS® game!

MOTHERLY LOVE

NOUN _____

ADJECTIVE _____

ADJECTIVE _____

NOUN _____

OCCUPATION _____

NOUN _____

ADJECTIVE _____

NOUN _____

VERB _____

ADJECTIVE _____

NOUN _____

PLURAL NOUN _____

MAD LIBS

MOTHERLY LOVE

Leonard's mother, Beverly Hofstadter, and Sheldon's _____,
                                                         NOUN

Mary Cooper, are very different. They are both _____ mothers
                                                   ADJECTIVE

who show their love in _____ ways.
                          ADJECTIVE

• Dr. Hofstadter is a/an _____-renowned neuro-_____
                             NOUN   OCCUPATION

and a/an _____-winning psychiatrist and author.
             NOUN

Mary Cooper is a/an _____, born-again _____
                         ADJECTIVE   NOUN

from East Texas.

• Mary Cooper is the only person who is able to make Sheldon

_____ when he does something wrong. Dr. Hofstadter is
      VERB

the only person who criticizes poor, _____ Leonard more
                                            ADJECTIVE

than Sheldon does!

• Dr. Hofstadter loves Sheldon more than she loves Leonard. And

Mary Cooper loves Sheldon more than anyone else, too (with the

exception of his twin _____, Missy). Looks like these
                             NOUN

two _____ have something in common, after all!
         PLURAL NOUN

MAD LIBS® is fun to play with friends, but you can also play it by yourself! To begin with, DO NOT look at the story on the page below. Fill in the blanks on this page with the words called for. Then, using the words you have selected, fill in the blank spaces in the story.

Now you've created your own hilarious MAD LIBS® game!

DRIVING WITH SHELDON

ADJECTIVE _____

NOUN _____

NOUN _____

NOUN _____

ADJECTIVE _____

VERB _____

SILLY WORD _____

NOUN _____

SAME NOUN _____

NOUN _____

NOUN _____

ADJECTIVE _____

NOUN _____

VERB _____

VERB ENDING IN "ING" _____

MAD LIBS

DRIVING WITH SHELDON

If you're _____ enough, you could be the unlucky
                ADJECTIVE

_____ who drives Sheldon to work, to the _____-
   NOUN   NOUN

book store, or to _____ Barn to return his Star Wars sheets.
                      NOUN

If you're stuck in the car with Sheldon, here are a few _____
                                                         ADJECTIVE

pieces of advice to make your ride go as smoothly as possible:

- Let him choose the road you _____ on. If you want
                                  VERB

  to take _____ Avenue, but Leonard usually takes
            SILLY WORD

  _____ Road, Sheldon will likely request that you take
     NOUN

  _____ Road also.
   SAME NOUN

- Make sure your car is fully inspected and there's no "check

  _____" light lit on your dashboard.
     NOUN

- If Sheldon wants to play the Periodic _____ Game, then
                                            NOUN

  you're going to have to play the game. No listening to loud and

  _____ music, either.
     ADJECTIVE

- Don't ask Sheldon to get his own driver's _____ and
                                                NOUN

  learn how to _____, because he's way too evolved for
                    VERB

  _____ on his own!
   VERB ENDING IN "ING"

MAD LIBS® is fun to play with friends, but you can also play it by yourself! To begin with, DO NOT look at the story on the page below. Fill in the blanks on this page with the words called for. Then, using the words you have selected, fill in the blank spaces in the story.

Now you've created your own hilarious MAD LIBS® game!

BERNADETTE IS BOSS

ADJECTIVE _____

COLOR _____

ADJECTIVE _____

ANIMAL _____

ARTICLE OF CLOTHING _____

NOUN _____

TYPE OF FOOD _____

PLURAL NOUN _____

NOUN _____

NOUN _____

ADJECTIVE _____

PART OF THE BODY _____

ARTICLE OF CLOTHING (PLURAL) _____

OCCUPATION _____

MAD LIBS®

BERNADETTE IS BOSS

Bernadette might look cute and _____, but don't let
                                    ADJECTIVE

her looks fool you. Underneath her shiny, _____ hair
                                              COLOR

and _____-pitched voice is a woman who is as fierce as
        ADJECTIVE

a/an _____! After all, she married Howard and manages to
        ANIMAL

make him think he wears the _____ in the family when
                              ARTICLE OF CLOTHING

everyone else knows the truth—that Bernadette is boss. How does she

manage to get her way while still looking so adorable? Here's how . . .

- Be really smart. Earn a degree in _____-biology while
                                        NOUN

  working at the _____ Factory. Then land a job that pays
                    TYPE OF FOOD

  you way more _____ than your husband's!
                  PLURAL NOUN

- Marry a Jewish _____ to rebel against your Catholic
                    NOUN

  mother and overprotective father.

- Marry a Jewish _____ to drive his mother crazy.
                    NOUN

- Look _____ and innocent on the outside by curling your
          ADJECTIVE

  _____ and wearing conservative _____,
  PART OF THE BODY   ARTICLE OF CLOTHING (PLURAL)

  but have a mouth like a/an _____!
                              OCCUPATION

Download Mad Libs today!

Join the millions of Mad Libs fans creating wacky and wonderful stories on our apps!